EXPLORING NATURE AROUND THE YEAR
SPRING

EXPLORING NATURE AROUND THE YEAR

SPRING

DAVID WEBSTER
PICTURES BY BARBARA STEADMAN

JULIAN MESSNER

Text copyright © 1990 by David Webster. Illustrations copyright © 1990 by Barbara Steadman. All rights reserved including the right of reproduction in whole or in part in any form. Published by Julian Messner, a division of Silver Burdett Press, Inc., Simon & Schuster, Inc. Prentice Hall Bldg., Englewood Cliffs, NJ 07632.

JULIAN MESSNER and colophon are trademarks of Simon & Schuster, Inc.

Design by Malle N. Whitaker.

Manufactured in the United States of America.

Lib. ed.   10 9 8 7 6 5 4 3 2 1

Paper ed. 10 9 8 7 6 5 4 3 2 1

Library of Congress Cataloging-in-Publication Data

Webster, David, 1930-
    Exploring nature around the year : spring / by David Webster.
      p. cm.
    Summary: A collection of activities and projects exploring nature in the spring.
    1. Spring—Juvenile literature. 2. Nature study—Juvenile literature. [1. Spring 2. Nature study.]
I. Steadman, Barbara, ill. II. Title
QH81.W46913 1990   508—dc20   89-14505
CIP   AC
ISBN   0-671-65858-1
ISBN   0-671-65983-9 (pbk.)

CONTENTS

INTRODUCTION	7
WEEDS AND SEEDS	10
Weed Seeds • Supermarket Seeds • Sprouting Birdseed • Transplanting Seedlings • Bigfoot Is Alive! • Your Pet Dandelion • Make a Terrarium	
POND LIFE	17
Make a Pond • Pond Animals and Plants • A Snorkel Viewer	
SIGNS OF ANIMALS	20
Can You Make a Bird Nest? • Help Birds Build Nests • A Bone Hunt • Dinner Bone Collection • Casts of Animal Tracks • Animals Are Messy Eaters	
WEATHER	27
Your Weather Station • Thermometer • Rain Gauge • Wind Vane • Wind Speed Meter • Clouds • Make a Cloud	
TREES	35
Tree Flowers • Tree Rings • Make a Branch Puzzle • Bark Rubbings • Big Trees	
ROCKS AND SOIL	41
Sand • Soil • Soil Water • Rock Collection	
A NATURE MUSEUM	46
INDEX	47

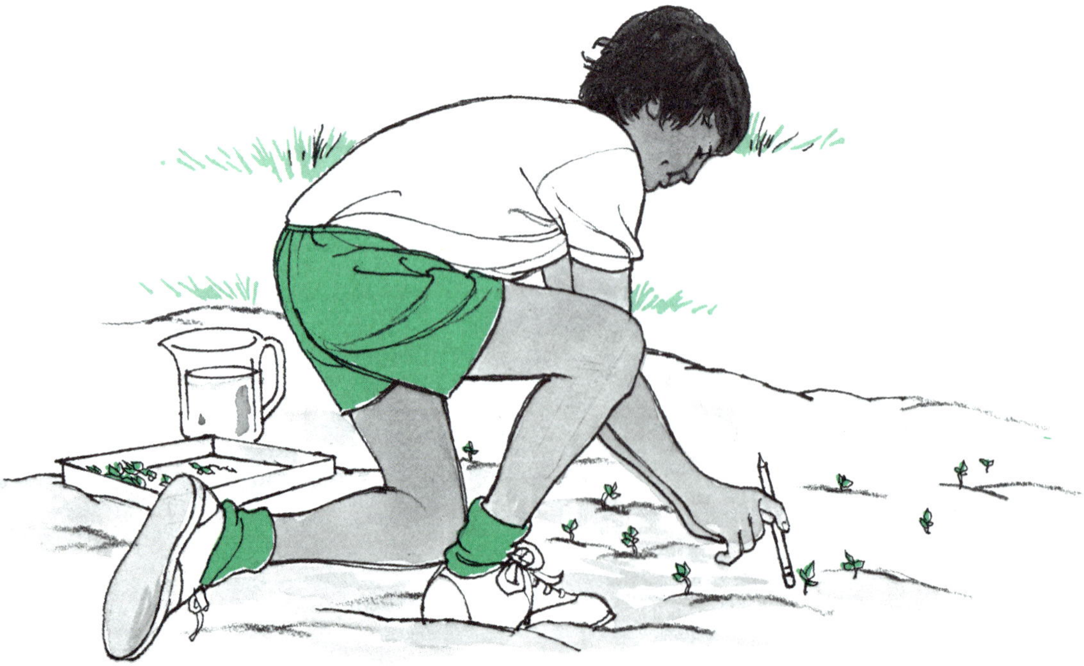

INTRODUCTION

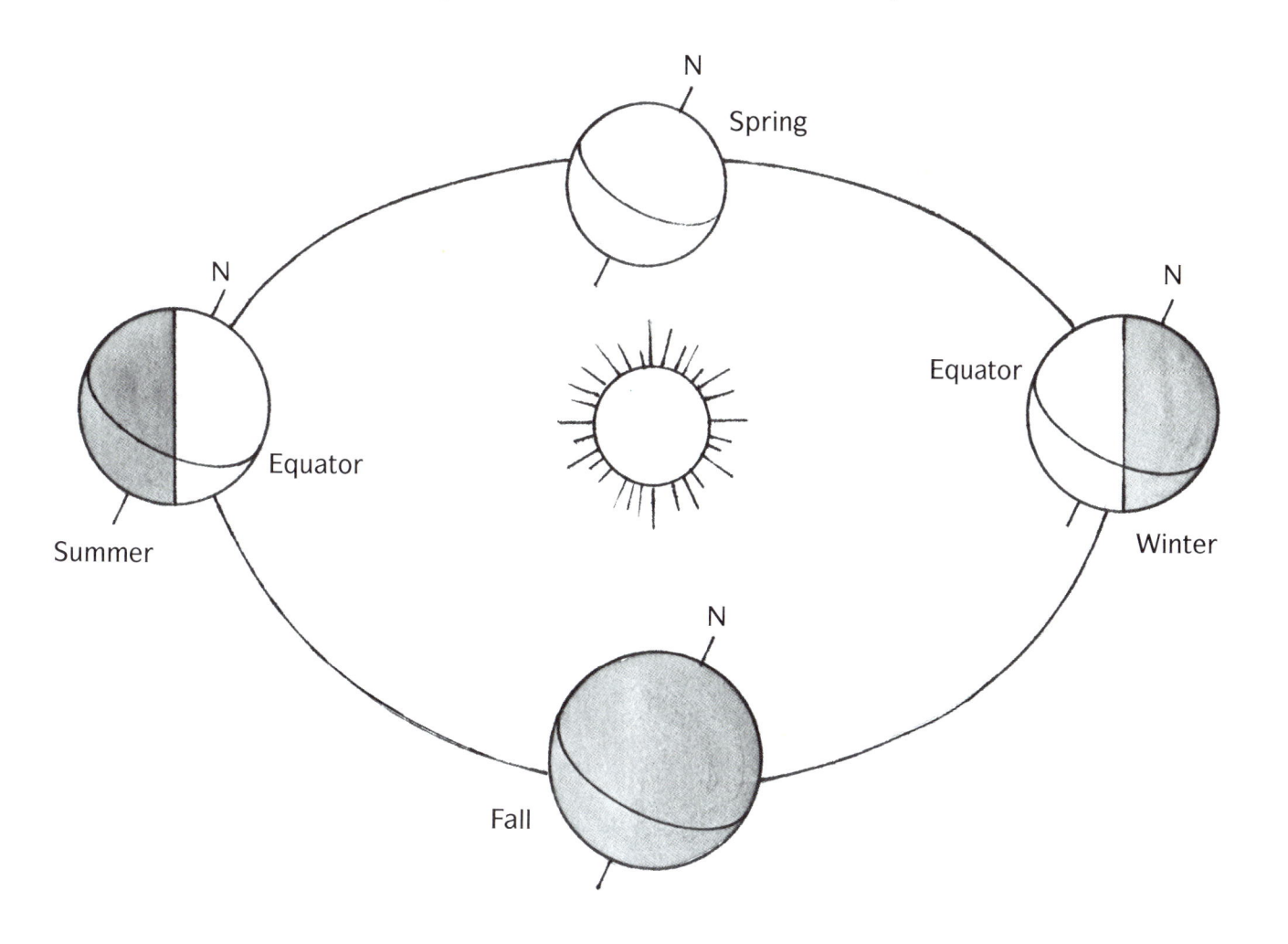

*"Spring, the sweet spring, is the year's pleasant king;
Then blooms each thing, then maids dance in a ring,
Cold doth not sting, the pretty birds do sing."*

So wrote the poet Thomas Nash about 400 years ago. Many people would agree that spring is their favorite season. Gone are winter's gray cold and the windy days of March. April welcomes animals and plants to a fresh awakening as the earth warms up.

Winter begins on the shortest day of the year, December 21. Gradually, throughout the winter, the days get longer. More daylight means more heat. When spring starts about March 21, the days and nights are of equal length. The longest day of the year comes when spring ends about June 21.

Usually plants are the first to signal the start of spring. Grass turns green and weed seeds sprout as warm rains soak into the soil. Tree buds split open; green leaves will soon fill the sky. Brighter colors glow from tiny tree flowers and golden dandelions.

Animals, too, greet the arrival of spring with renewed activity. Hibernating animals emerge from their deep sleep, and many birds migrate north, since food will again be plentiful. Soon birds are busy with nest building, and furry animals start new families.

For people, spring might mean washing the car, spring cleaning, starting the garden, celebrating Easter or Passover, walking in the park, jumping rope, riding a bike, fishing, and playing baseball.

8

Spring is a perfect season to go outside for nature and science activities. If you like gardening, you can sprout seeds to start a flower or vegetable garden. Or you can study the slow growth of trees by counting their growth rings.

There are lots of other projects that involve animals. Birds appreciate special things you can provide for nest-building materials. It is fun to make a collection of tracks that animals leave in the soft spring mud. Also, you can start an aquarium with tiny water creatures captured in a pond or swamp.

Your springtime weather activities could include making a rain gauge and wind vane for a weather station, or learning how to predict weather by watching the clouds.

No matter where you live, there are animals, plants, rocks, and clouds waiting for you. Go outside whenever you can and explore the fascinating world of nature in the spring!

9

WEEDS AND SEEDS

WEED SEEDS

Almost all soil contains tiny weed seeds waiting to sprout when the soil warms in the spring. You can make seeds germinate, or sprout, early by bringing some soil inside.

All you need is a garden trowel or old spoon for digging, and a few waxed paper cups. Use a pencil point to punch a few small holes in the bottom of each cup.

Find a place in your yard or a park where you can dig up a little soil. Sunny areas are best; weeds do not grow well in the dark woods. Pack some soil into a cup until it is almost full. Get soil for other cups from different places.

You can keep the cups of soil in your room on saucers or in a shallow pan. Water the soil every day to keep it damp but not muddy. If the soil does get too wet, the water will drain out of the holes.

Look in the soil every day for tiny seedlings. How soon can you tell if your weeds are the same or different? Can you grow a weed 6 inches tall?

SUPERMARKET SEEDS

Seeds	Color	Size	Shape	Name
	Brown	Small	Oblong	Celery
	Brown	Medium	Round with Lines	Coriander
	White	Medium	Pickle	Rice
	Dark Red	Large	Frisbee	Lentil
	Dark Brown	Medium	Round, Crinkled	Pepper
	Beige	Medium	Round, Smooth	Mustard

It is easy to make a seed collection with seeds from a supermarket. For making soups, there are dried beans, peas, lentils, and barley. In the spice section you can find lots of little seeds: anise, caraway, poppy, sesame, mustard, dill, celery, fennel, and peppercorns. You may have some of these in your kitchen already.

Make up a poster for your seed collection. Samples of each kind of seed can be glued to the paper. In spaces beside the seeds you can describe their color, size, and shape. A magnifying glass will help you see more differences. Write the seeds' names in the last column.

See if your friends can figure out what kinds of seeds you have. Cover up the names with another piece of paper before you let them guess.

Ask your mother or father if you can taste a few of the leftover spice seeds. Maybe you can help make soup with some of the dried beans or peas.

SPROUTING BIRDSEED

What does a seed need to germinate, or sprout? Just like most living things, seeds must have water and warmth to start growing. Does a seed also need light to germinate? Is there any light under the soil where seeds usually sprout?

You can watch seeds sprout in a germination chamber. All you need is some birdseed from the supermarket, a paper towel, and a wide-mouthed jar or plastic container. Cut several circles from the paper towel and place them in the bottom of the container. Put a little water in the container, and then pour the water out. Seeds should sprout well on the moist towel.

Drop in different kinds of seeds from the birdseed or other supermarket seeds. Cover the top of the container with a piece of plastic wrap so the towel does not become dry.

Look at the seeds every day. How will you know when a seed has sprouted? Do you think every seed will germinate? Add a few drops of water if the towel dries out.

TRANSPLANTING SEEDLINGS

Of course, seedlings cannot grow for long with just warmth and water. They soon need light from the sun and minerals from the soil. They must be transplanted.

Ask if you can plant your seedlings in a small garden in your yard. If you have no yard, the seedlings could be planted in flower pots or large cups. The cups should be kept on a windowsill that gets some sunlight. Seedlings will grow better outside, however.

You must not plant seedlings outside too early. In northern areas, wait until late April or May, after the danger of frost.

Handle the seedlings carefully; such small plants are delicate. Use a pencil to make small holes in the soil. Set the seedlings in the holes. With the pencil eraser, pack soil gently around the seedlings. Water them every day unless it rains.

If you take good care of your seedlings, they might grow big and tall by the end of the summer. Maybe you will be lucky and get some flowers and vegetables.

BIGFOOT IS ALIVE!

Have you ever heard of Bigfoot? Bigfoot is the huge, furry animal-man that some people think lives in remote mountain areas. You can make Bigfoot come alive with a big sponge and some grass seed.

Get a large sponge and ask an adult to help cut it with scissors into a human shape. Lay the cut sponge in a shallow pan and pour in water. The top of the sponge should be out of the water.

Grass seed can be bought in a hardware, garden supply, or farm feed store. Sprinkle a thick layer of seed over the top of the wet sponge.

Look at Bigfoot every day. How can you tell when the seeds sprout and begin to grow? Soon Bigfoot should be covered with green "hair."

Put Bigfoot near a window. The grass will start to bend over as it grows toward the light. In a few days, turn Bigfoot around to make the grass bend in the other direction. How tall will the grass grow?

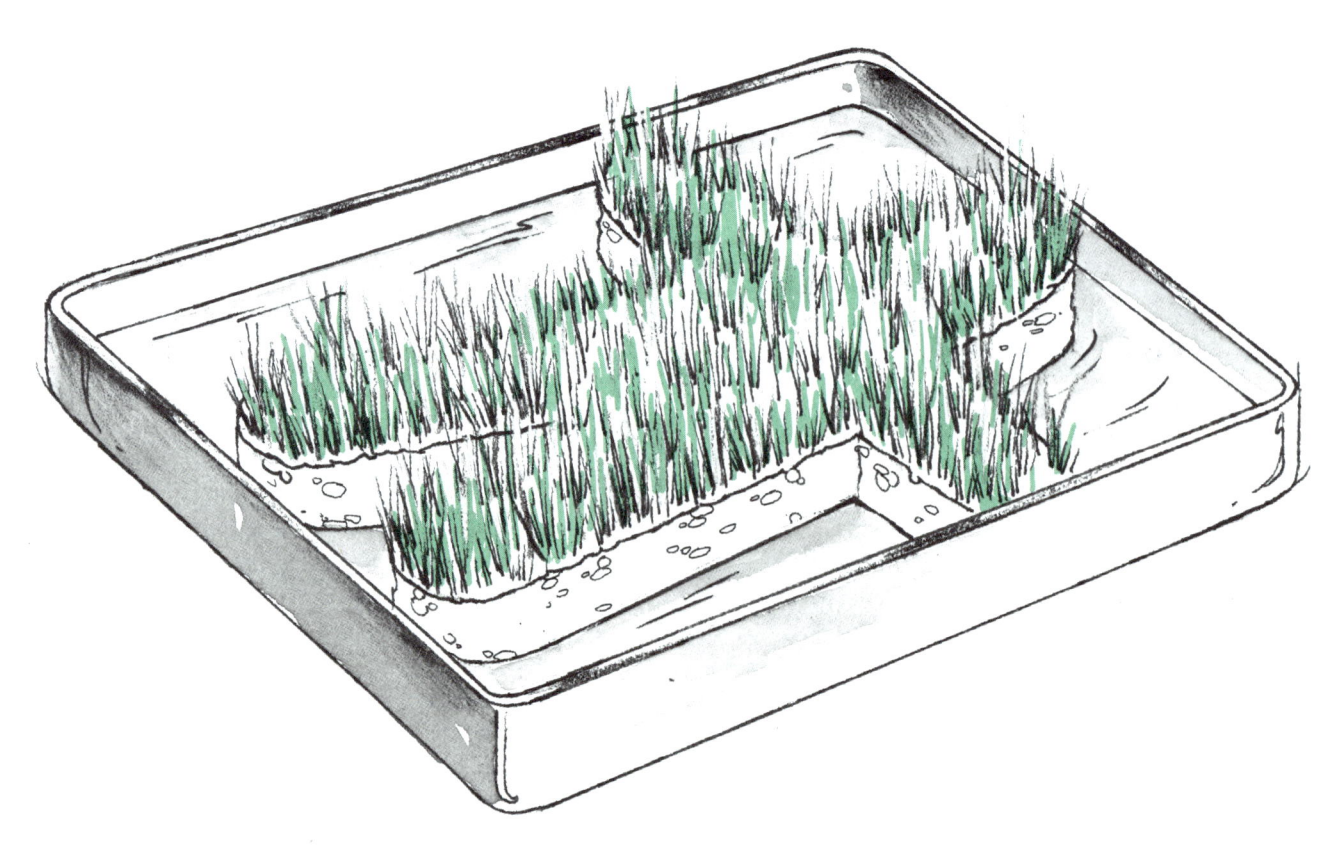

YOUR PET DANDELION

Do dandelions grow where you live? In most places, yellow dandelion flowers appear in the spring in many lawns and fields. If you can find a dandelion plant, claim it as your Special Pet Flower. Push a pencil or stick into the soil next to your plant so you can always find it.

Look at the dandelion as soon as you get up in the morning. Is the flower opened up? Check it again in the evening before dark. After the sun sets, use a flashlight to see if the flower has closed up. Dandelion flowers shut up tightly during the night.

Dandelion flowers also turn slowly during the day, following the sun. Look at your flower in the morning on a sunny day. Lay a pencil on the ground pointing toward the center of the flower. Go back in the afternoon and see if the flower has moved.

When the flower begins to die, cut off its stem close to the ground. Pull the flower off the top, and look at the stem. Is it hollow like a straw? Use the hollow flower stalk to drink some milk from a glass.

MAKE A TERRARIUM

A terrarium is a tiny garden growing inside a jar. The jar should have a cap and be wide enough for you to reach in. For digging you will need a garden trowel or an old spoon. Pack about an inch of soil into the bottom of the jar.

You should be able to find terrarium plants in your yard, the school playground, a park, or a vacant lot. Be sure to get permission before you dig up any plants. And always have extra soil to fill in the holes you make. Look for small plants, no more than a few inches high. Put in three or four different kinds. Some moss would look nice covering the bare spots.

Sprinkle in a little water, and put the cap on the jar. Keep the terrarium on a windowsill that gets some sun. Add a little more water if the soil becomes dry.

What will happen when a plant grows tall and reaches the top? How long will the plants live?

POND LIFE

MAKE A POND

You can make a pond for water animals in a plastic wading pool. The pool should be placed in the shade under a tree or on an open porch.

Cover the bottom of the pool with clean gravel. Dirty or dusty gravel should be washed with a hose or rinsed in a bucket before it is put in. Place a few large rocks in the pool to serve as underwater hiding places and above-water resting spots for the animals.

Fill your little pond about halfway with water from a hose or buckets. Let the water sit for a few days to allow any harmful chemicals to escape into the air.

If you cannot use a wading pool, you could still make a pond in your house in an aquarium, dishpan, or large jar. Set up your indoor pond in the same way as a wading pool, using gravel, a rock, and water.

POND ANIMALS AND PLANTS

For catching pond creatures you should have a dip net. You can make one by taping a large kitchen strainer to a pole or green stick. Bend back the strainer's "ears" and flatten the rim so it is flat on the top.

For carrying home your finds, you need a plastic container with a top. A bucket is also useful to hold larger animals and water plants.

What animals can you get from a pond or swamp? Hiding on the bottom might be tadpoles, minnows, insect nymphs, crayfish, leeches, or snails. If you are lucky, you might catch a frog or turtle. In early spring, look for floating frog and toad eggs. Keep larger animals in your pool for only a few days. Then let them go free in the pond where you found them.

Many pond animals are almost too small to see. Sort through a netful of leaves and muck from the pond bottom. Look for tiny insects, water fleas, and pill clams.

Some water plants will make your homemade pond look more like a real one. Maybe you can dig up a few small plants from the shallow water. Some kinds of pond plants have no roots; they float on the surface.

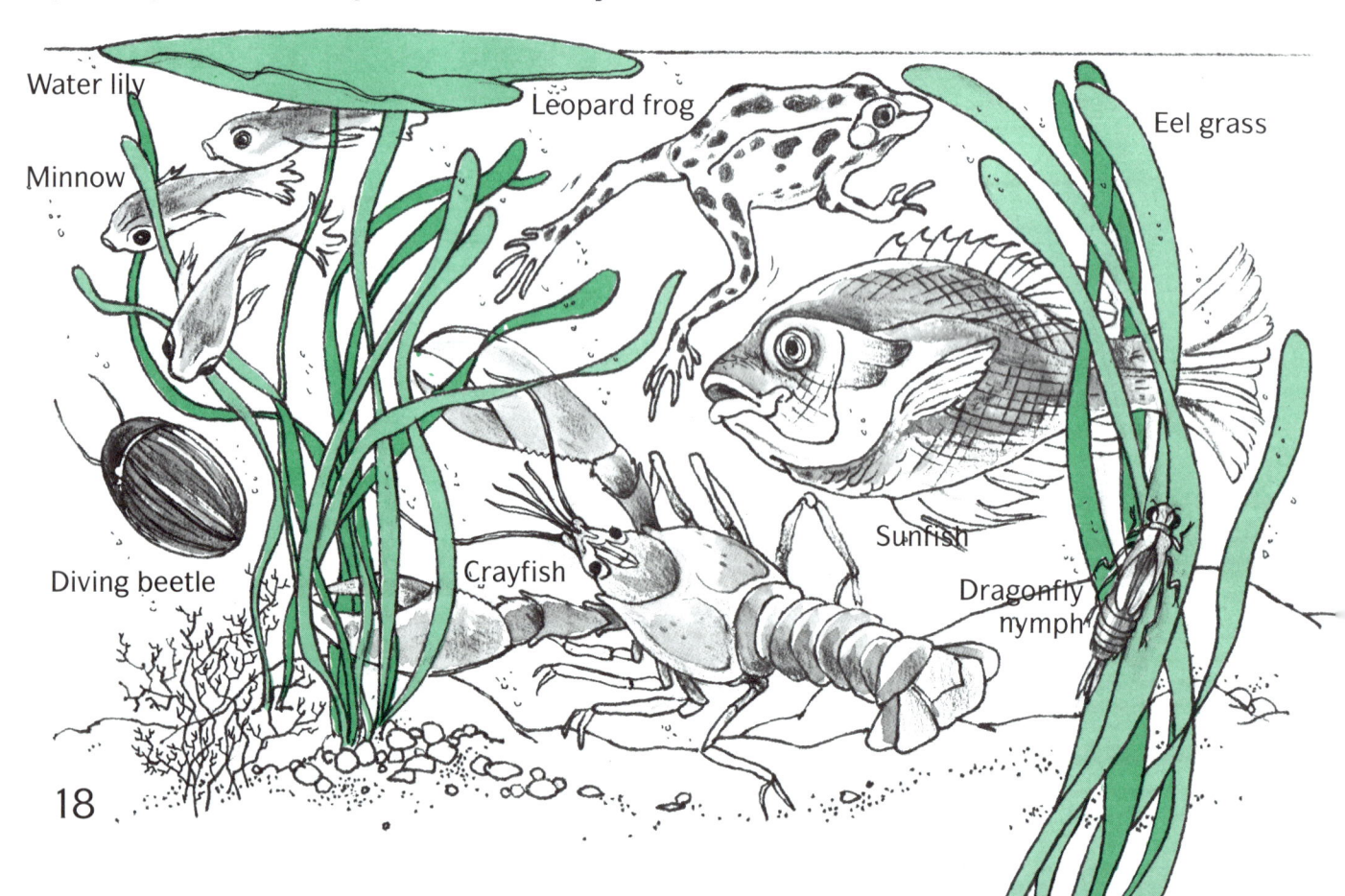

A SNORKEL VIEWER

You need not worry about feeding your pond animals. Frogs, fish, and insects are cold-blooded, and do not need nearly as much food as warm-blooded birds and mammals. Many smaller animals will eat algae and decaying plants.

You can watch pond animals better with a Snorkel Viewer. Have an adult help you cut out the bottom of a plastic container, making a hole slightly smaller than the bottom. Then cover the hole and sides of the container with a large piece of plastic food wrap. Hold the plastic wrap in place with several large rubber bands.

Use the snorkel viewer to watch animals in your pond. Push the viewer partway under the water. Keep the inside of the container dry. The pressure of the water pushes the plastic upward in the shape of a large lens. The lens magnifies the water animals and makes them look larger.

Can you see any animals searching for food on the bottom? Look for tiny water beetles and hair worms. If you have a fish, watch how it moves its fins.

SIGNS OF ANIMALS

CAN YOU MAKE A BIRD NEST?

Have you ever tried to make a bird nest? It is not easy.

Many birds weave a nest from straw: dead pieces of long grass and thin weed stems. Look for straw in a field or along the edges of your yard where the grass is not mowed. Cut off the straw with a pair of scissors until you have a handful.

Now turn the wad of straw around and around in your hands. Try to form it into a donut shape by using your thumbs to hollow out the middle.

Most birds use softer materials to line the inside of the nest. Look for soft leaves, pine needles, or dead flower fuzz.

Is your nest very strong? Drop it on a table and see if it stays together. Who can make a better bird nest, you or a bird?

Birds make strong nests without tools or hands. They have only their beaks and skinny feet. And no one ever taught birds how to make nests; they just do it.

HELP BIRDS BUILD NESTS

Birds build nests in the early spring. Robins make nests from dead grass and mud, while other birds use dried rootlets, strips of birch bark, pine needles, or even horse hair.

It is hard for birds to find the nest materials they need. It would be nice for you to help them.

Build a small square with four pieces of wood. Cover the opening with a piece of 1/4-inch hardware cloth from a hardware store. Fill the rack with different materials used by birds. Stuff in pieces of dried grass, colored yarn, string, cotton, and strips of paper. Then hang the rack from a tree branch you can see from inside your house.

It will take the birds a while to find the rack, so be patient. Watch the rack from your house whenever you have a few minutes. Even if you never see a bird taking something, you can tell birds have visited if the materials start to disappear.

When fall comes, look for bird nests in trees and bushes around your house. Maybe you can find a nest made with some of your materials.

A BONE HUNT

Have you ever found a bone outside? When a wild animal dies, its flesh usually is eaten by scavengers: animals such as crows, raccoons, dogs, and certain kinds of beetles. Bacteria consume the remaining flesh, leaving the bones to bleach white in the rain and sun.

Go on a bone hunt in a field or woods, the school yard, or a park. You will need sharp eyes. Walk around slowly, looking for white bones partly hidden by dead leaves or the soil.

If you find a bone, try to figure out what animal it came from. A skull or jaw has the shape of the animal's head. Teeth tell what the animal ate. Rodents have large front incisors for gnawing bark and seeds. Meat-eaters have large fangs and pointed molars for ripping flesh.

A long bone probably is from a leg. Think about the length of animals' legs. Would your legbone be the right size for a squirrel, a dog, or a crow? Smaller bones with holes might be pieces of the backbone. Ribs are thin, curved bones, and a flat bone could be a shoulder blade or hip bone.

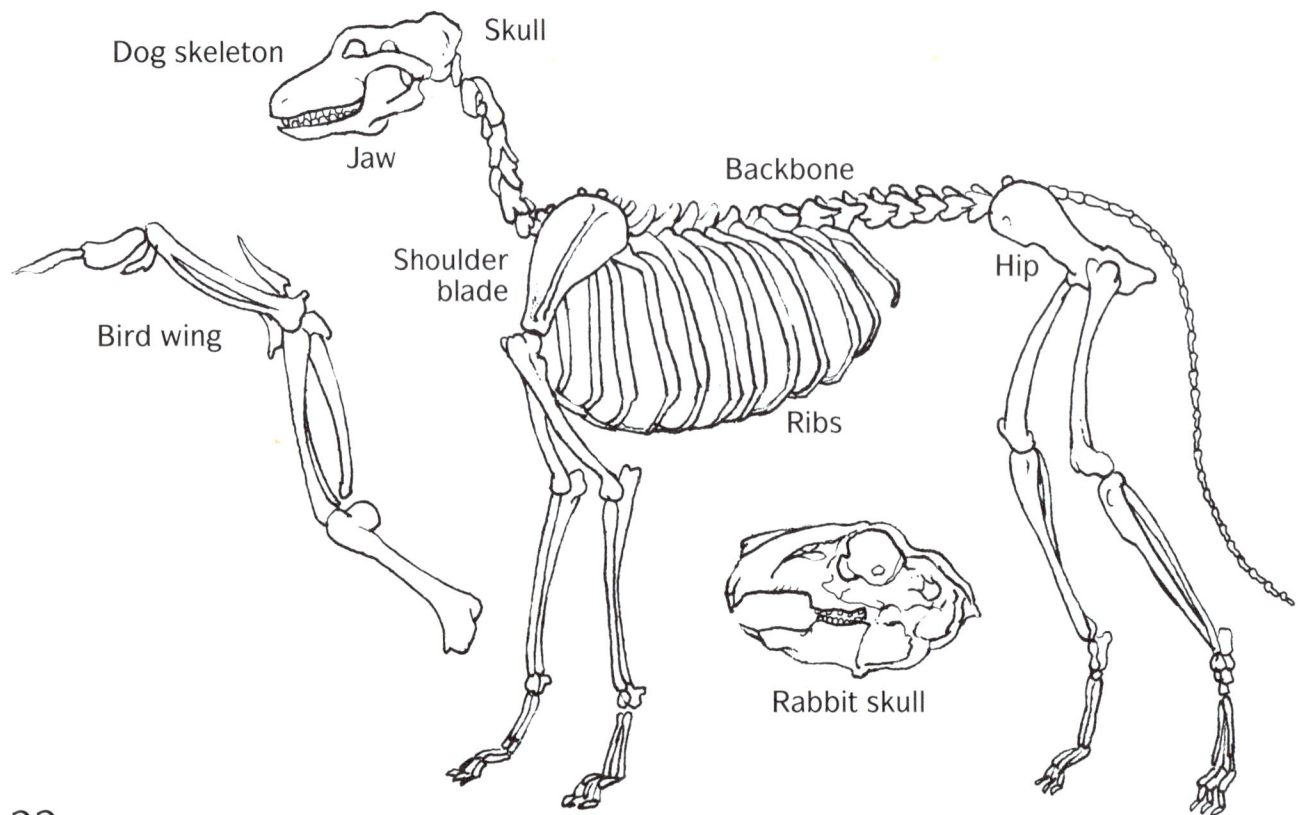

DINNER BONE COLLECTION

The bones you probably know best are the ones left on your dinner table. Steaks, chops, and roasts usually have pieces of bones that have been cut by the butcher. Whole bones are left after a meal of fried chicken, roast turkey, or baked fish.

Start saving bones from your dinners for a bone collection. Boil the bones in hot water. After they cool, scrape off the meat and gristle with your fingernails. Lay the bones on an old newspaper for a few days until they dry out.

You might be able to identify dinner bones by their shape. A roast leg of lamb has a long, thick leg bone. The round bone from a slice of ham is part of the leg bone cut crosswise. The funny-shaped piece of bone in a chop or steak is from the animal's backbone.

You can make a display of your clean bones for others to study. See if your friends can guess what kind of meat each bone came from.

Lamb chop

Pork shoulder

Beef short rib

Chicken leg

Ham steak

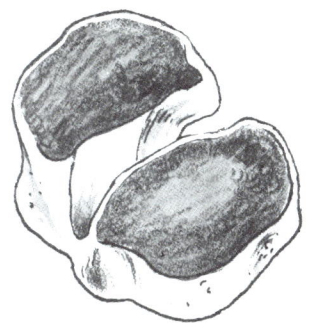

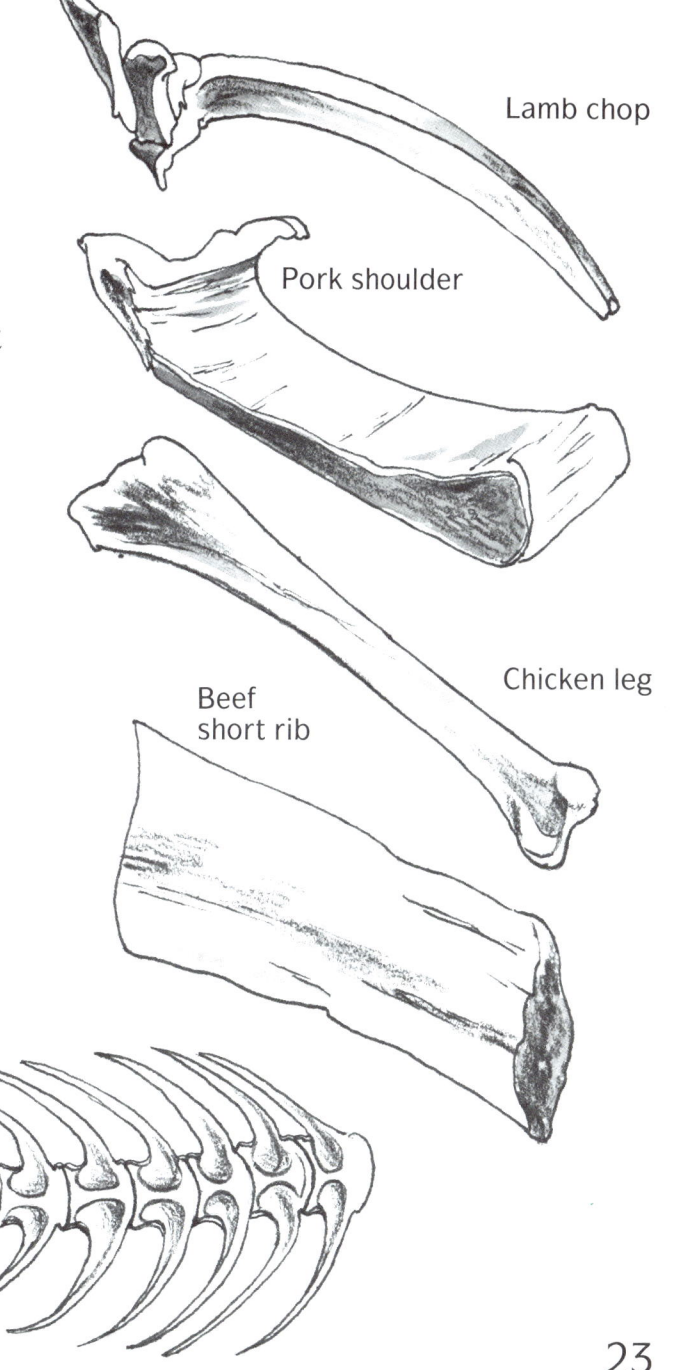

Fish

23

CASTS OF ANIMAL TRACKS

Most wild animals do not like you to see them. Often the only way you know they are around is when you notice their tracks.

Spring is a good time to look for tracks. Melting snow and spring rains turn bare soil into squishy mud. Look for tracks by a stream or pond, or where the grass is worn away along a driveway or sidewalk.

For making track casts, or copies, you will need plaster of Paris, water, a large plastic container for mixing, and an old spoon. You can buy plaster of Paris in a hardware store.

Since the plaster hardens quickly, it cannot be mixed until you find a nice track. Put four handfuls of plaster in the mixing container. Slowly add water while you mix with the old spoon. For casting, the plaster should be about as thick as melted ice cream. If you put in too much water, add more plaster.

Pour the plaster into the track. After several hours, lift the hardened plaster from the mud and wash it under running water.

Try to find tracks of other animals so you can make more casts.

24

Squirrel

front

hind

Cat

Crow

Dog

Skunk

These track drawings will help you identify some of the ones you find. Usually dog tracks are the most common. Squirrel and rabbit tracks are different from other animals; hopping animals have hind feet much larger than front feet. The four skinny toes of a bird track make it easy to recognize.

Dogs and cats walk on tiptoe and have small heel pads. Animals that walk flat-footed have large heel pads. Does a skunk walk flat-footed or on tiptoe? Look at your own bare feet as you walk on tiptoe and in the regular way.

ANIMALS ARE MESSY EATERS

The messy eating habits of most animals can help you find signs of hidden wildlife. Squirrels leave piles of cracked acorns and other nuts in places where they sit to feed. They eat the soft nut meats and leave the shells behind. Pine cones are a favorite food of red squirrels. Look for chewed up pine cones on top of rocks and logs.

During the winter, mice, rabbits, and porcupines often chew the bark from saplings and branches of larger trees. The gnawed spots show up because the wood under the bark is white and smooth.

A scattering of feathers is a sure sign of a cat-and-bird battle. A bird has little chance against a cat's needlelike nails and fangs.

Skunks use their long nails to search for insects and grubs in the soil. Look for small, round holes in the grass or in needles under pine trees.

Woodpeckers hammer off tree bark in search of insects hiding underneath. A sapsucker makes lines of holes in the bark of trees such as apple and aspen. The bird checks the holes later, hoping to find insects stuck in the sap that oozes from the holes.

WEATHER

YOUR WEATHER STATION

Weather Chart

Day	Time	Temperature	Wind Speed	Wind Direction	Cloud Type	Rainfall
Monday	4:00 P.M.	78°F	5 m.p.h.	South	Cirrus	0
Tuesday	4:30 P.M.	76°F	8 m.p.h.	South	Cumulus	0.2 in.
Wednesday	8:30 A.M.	62°F	20 m.p.h.	West	None	0
Thursday	8:15 A.M.	51°F	5 m.p.h.	North	Stratus	0
Friday						
Saturday						
Sunday						

You've probably heard lots of weather forecasts on the radio or TV. Weather reporters study special instruments before they make their predictions. But even with fancy equipment, the weather experts still make many mistakes.

You can start a weather station to learn more about the weather. The best instruments to have are a thermometer, a rain gauge, a wind vane, and a wind speed meter. There are suggestions for making and using these on the next pages. Watching clouds is another way to study weather.

Practice writing down the information you get from your weather instruments. Make a chart like the one in the picture. Then maybe you can begin to make your own weather predictions.

THERMOMETER

Probably the thing you notice most about weather is the temperature. You may already have an outdoor thermometer outside your house. If not, ask if you can buy one in a hardware store. Hang the thermometer in a shady place, and make daily readings. You may need help learning how to read the temperature properly.

Thermometers have two main types of number scales: Fahrenheit and Celsius. Most weather reports give the air temperature in Fahrenheit. Scientists working in chemistry labs measure temperature in Celsius.

Whenever you write down a temperature, you must include two things after the number. If you read 68 on your thermometer, you should write 68°F. The little circle stands for degrees and the letter "F" is for Fahrenheit. The proper way to say that temperature is "sixty-eight degrees Fahrenheit."

Pick a day to take temperature readings at many times. Start when you get up in the morning and make six to ten readings before bedtime. Remember to record the temperatures on a chart. At what time was it warmest? Why is it usually coolest in the morning?

28

RAIN GAUGE

A rain gauge is just a container for catching rain water. You can make one with a wide-mouthed jar. Peanut butter and mayonnaise come in nice large jars.

Put the jar outside in an open spot away from trees and buildings. The rain gauge should be tied to a wooden stake so it is not upset by the wind or a thirsty dog. You should check the gauge every day even if you have not seen rain. You might not know if there was rain while you were asleep.

To measure the rain in the jar, you need a special ruler. Get a thin stick about six inches long. A Popsicle stick is the right size. Use a desk ruler to mark off six inches on the stick. Then have someone help you divide each inch into ten equal spaces. Each space is one tenth of an inch.

At first, you may need help to measure the depth of rain water in the jar. Remember to record the amount of rainfall on your daily weather chart.

29

WIND VANE

A wind vane tells the direction of the wind. The drawing shows how to make a simple wind vane. Ask an adult to help you cut the arrow from a thin piece of wood. The wind vane should be attached to a post with a thin screw. Drill a hole through the wind vane at its balance point. The hole should be a little larger than the screw so the arrow can turn. The washer under the wind vane helps it to spin easier.

To describe wind direction, you must know the compass points of north, east, south, and west. A compass is the best way to find these directions. But without a compass, you can locate south with the sun. At noon, the sun is always toward the south and your shadow points north.

The wind vane will point in the direction from which the wind blows. If the arrow points toward the south, there is a south wind.

Enter each day's wind direction on your weather chart.

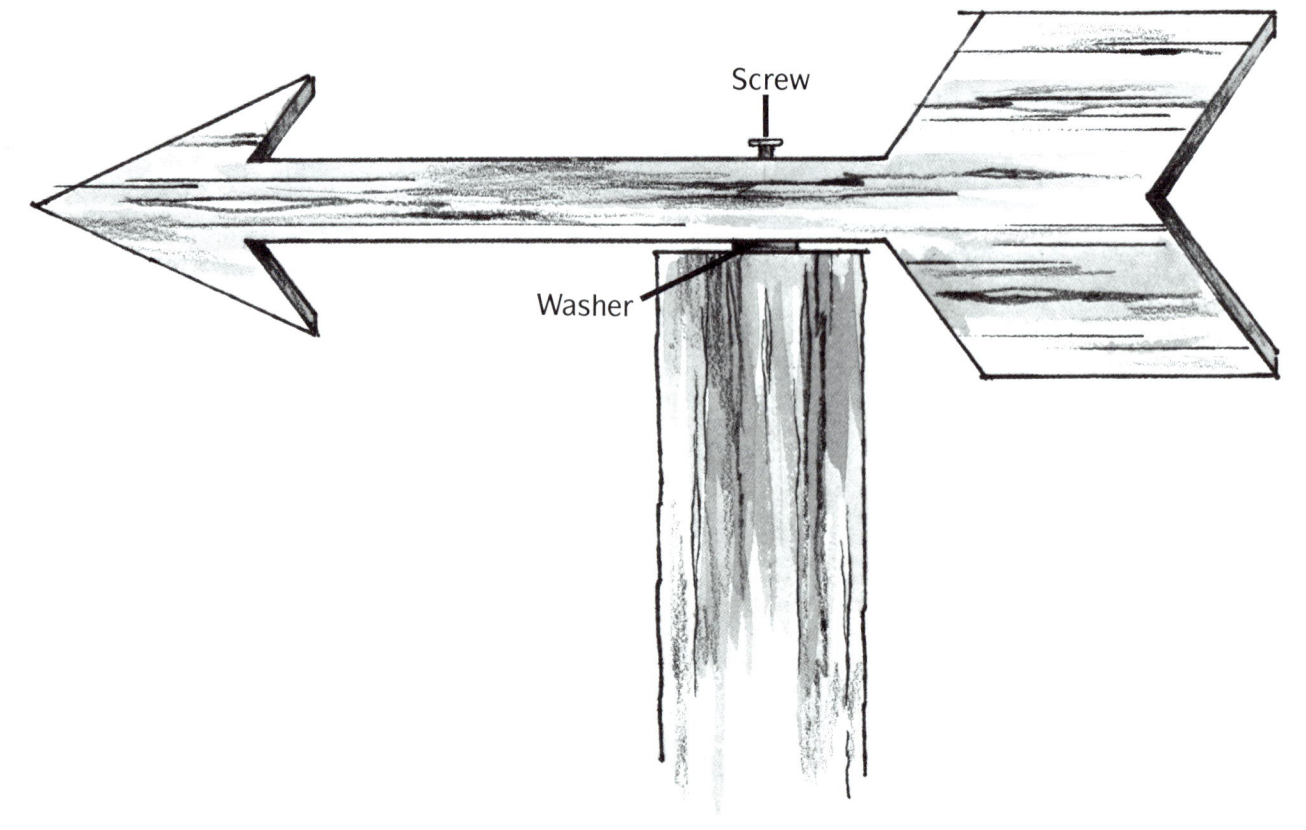

WIND SPEED METER

Weather reports usually give both wind direction and wind speed. You can build a simple meter to measure wind speed. A real wind speed meter is called an anemometer.

You need a small piece of wood about 6 inches square. Ask an adult friend to help you hammer nails part-way into two of the corners. Ask the friend to cut a strip of metal 8 inches long and 1 inch wide from a large tin can. Bend one end of the strip around one nail so the strip hangs freely.

To mark the speed scale, someone will have to take you for a short car ride on a day when there is no wind. Ask the driver to go exactly 10 miles per hour (MPH). Hold the wind speed meter out the window with the arrow facing into the wind. Mark the position of the metal strip with a line and the number 10. Make more marks with the car going 20, 30, 40, and 50 MPH.

When you use your wind speed meter, hold it straight up with the arrow facing into the wind. Read the scale and record the wind speed on your weather chart.

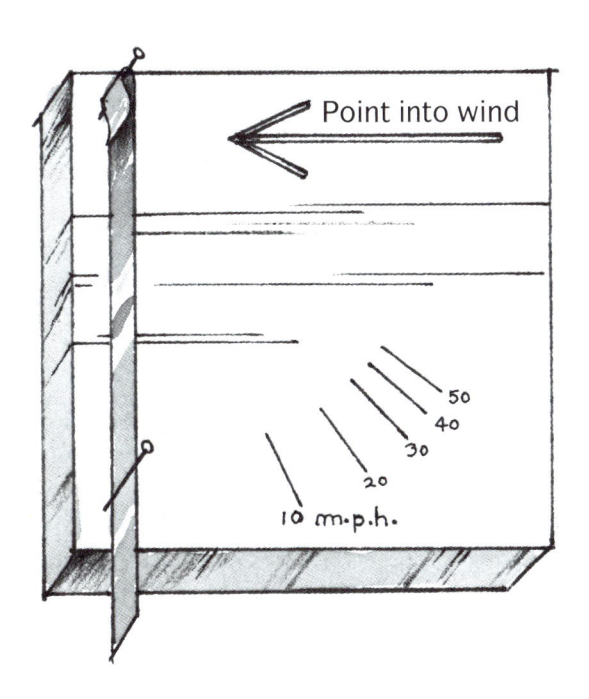

Anemometer

31

CLOUDS

Often the quickest way to find out about the weather is to look up at the clouds.

There are three main types of clouds: cirrus, cumulus, and stratus. Cirrus clouds look like wispy feathers and are about 4 miles high. The temperature at that height is so cold that the water droplets in the clouds usually are frozen into tiny ice crystals. With cirrus clouds you can expect fair weather to continue unless the clouds thicken. If cirrus clouds cover the whole sky, it means there probably will be rain in the next 24 hours.

Sometimes cirrus clouds form a banded pattern known as "mackerel sky." The clouds look like the dark bands of scales on a mackerel fish. If you see a mackerel sky, remember this weather poem:

> Mackerel sky:
> Never long wet;
> Never long dry.

Cumulus clouds

Cumulus clouds are the puffy, white clouds you see floating overhead on nice days. As long as cumulus clouds stay small, good weather will continue. Sometimes, though, cumulus clouds swell and darken to create huge thunderheads. Have you ever been scared by thunder and lightning during a storm?

Stratus clouds are layers of flat, grayish clouds. Dark stratus clouds are a sign of steady rain. Fog is a stratus cloud close to the ground.

MAKE A CLOUD

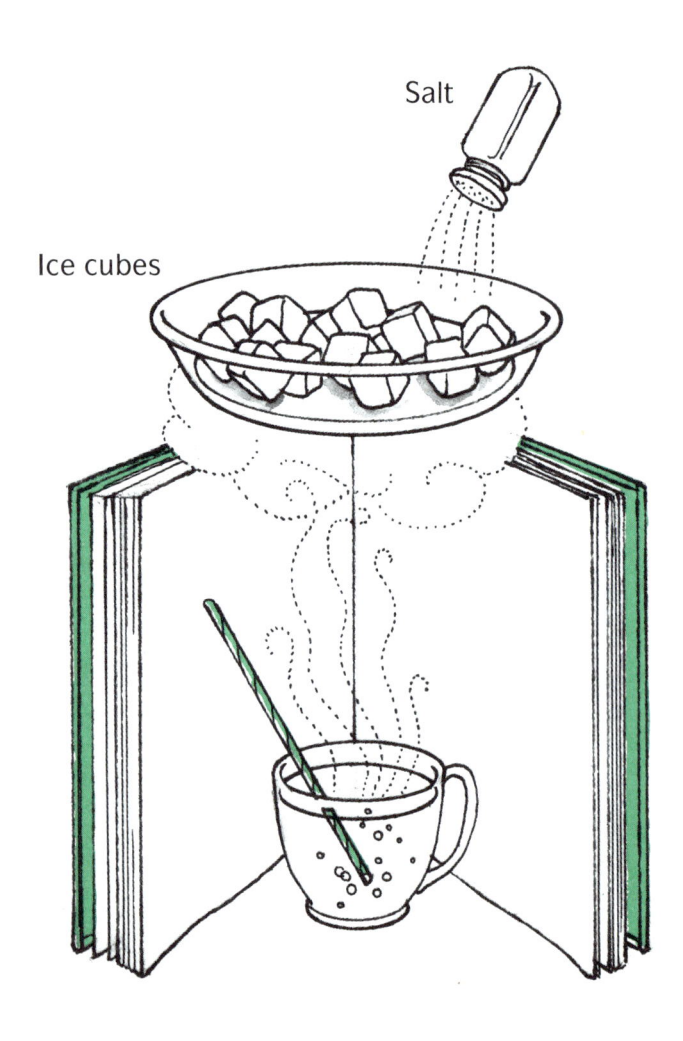

A cloud is just a huge blob of tiny water droplets floating in the air.

To see how a cloud is made, hold your mouth close to a mirror and blow softly. Tiny water droplets form when your warm, moist breath hits the cold glass. This is called condensation.

Here is a way to make a cloud:

1. Put some ice cubes in a metal or glass pie pan, and make the ice colder by sprinkling salt on it.

2. Use an opened book to hold the pie pan about 8 or 10 inches above a table.

3. Fill a coffee cup with very hot water.

4. Use a straw to blow through the hot water. A small cloud should form when the warm, moist air reaches the cold pie plate.

Real clouds happen in the same way. Warm, moist air above a lake or the ocean rises and meets cold air above.

TREES

TREE FLOWERS

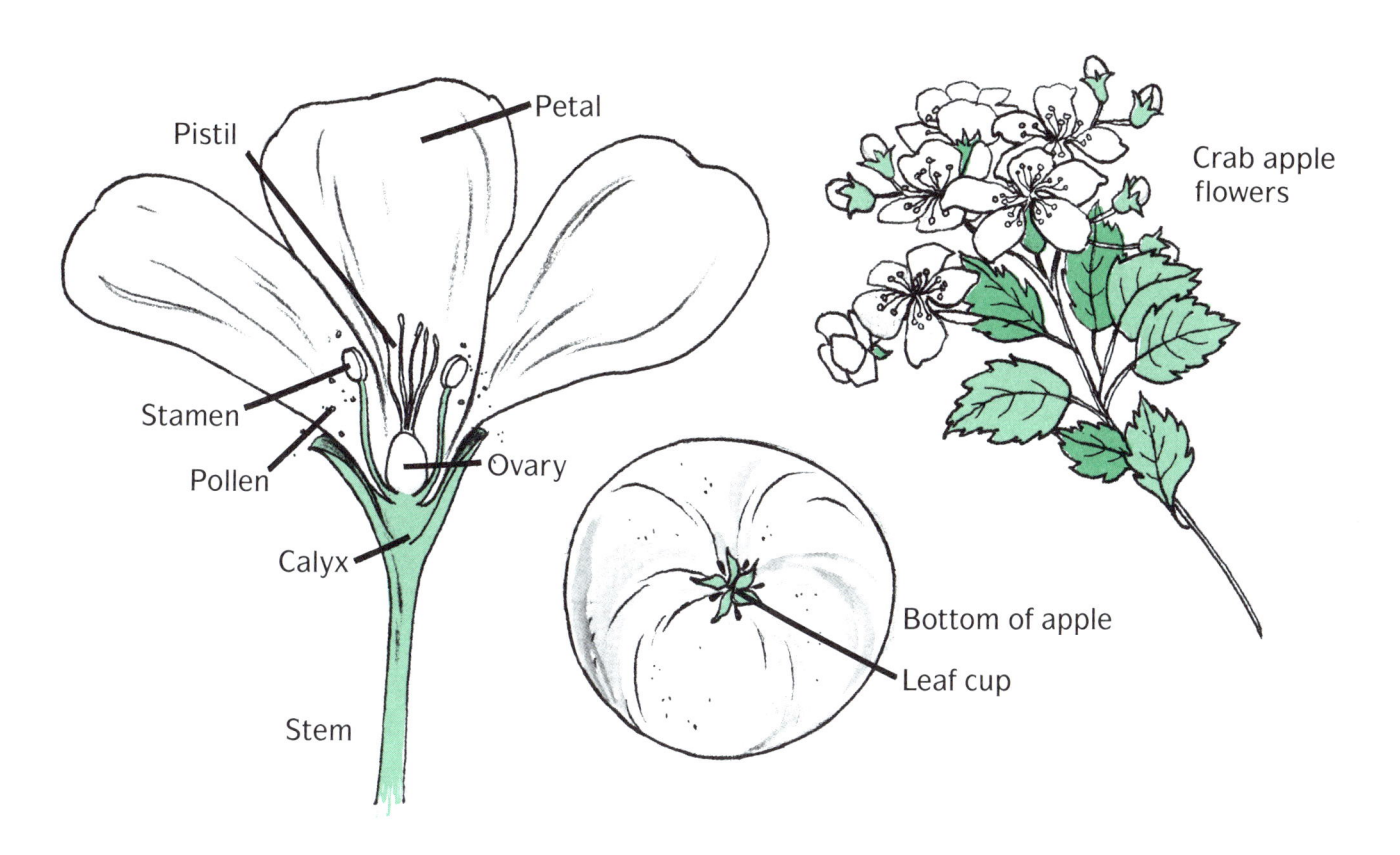

Everyone knows that plants have flowers. But did you know that most trees have flowers, too?

Look for tree flowers in the spring. The tiny red flowers on maple trees come out even before the green leaves. Apple and other fruit trees have much prettier flowers. Find a thin branch that is beginning to blossom, and ask if you can cut it off. Keep the branch in a jar of water so you can watch the flowers bloom. Tree flowers do not last long.

A tree must have flowers in order to produce seeds. Flower pollen is carried from tree to tree by bees or the wind. After the flower petals die, seeds develop slowly inside the ovary.

Every apple carries traces of its beginning in the apple tree flower. Look in the dent on the bottom of an apple. You will see five tiny points: the remains of the leaf cup that once held the flower.

TREE RINGS

Trees grow just like you do, only faster. In 20 years, a pine tree can reach 25 feet. How tall will you be when you are 20? Unlike you, trees never stop growing as they age.

You can tell the age of a tree by counting its yearly growth rings. The tree adds a new ring every year. The wide part of each ring forms as the tree grows quickly in March and April. The slow growth during the rest of the year makes a thin, dark ring.

If you know where a tree has been cut down, go and look at the stump. Can you see the rings? Count them by starting from the center of the stump. Is the tree older than you are?

Another place to find tree rings is on firewood. If you or a friend have a woodpile, look for rings on unsplit logs. You also can see growth rings on the cut ends of the lumber used to build houses.

With a saw, you can find tree rings yourself by cutting down a small tree. You could also cut off a low branch from a large tree. Of course, never cut down a tree or branch unless you have permission from the owner, and ask an adult to help with the sawing. Guess how old the tree is before sawing.

Tree rings can tell you more than just the tree's age. Wide rings mean fast growth, and narrow rings mean slow growth. Look at the picture of the pine stump. Did the pine grow faster when it was young or faster in the last years before it was cut down?

What can make a tree grow slowly? Trees do not grow well if the spring weather is too dry or too cold. Tree growth also can be slowed by diseases, attacks from insect pests, forest fires, and crowding by larger trees.

Study the picture of the oak stump. The tree was 18 years old when it was cut down in 1980. Can you tell what years had bad weather?

Try to figure out stories told by tree rings you find.

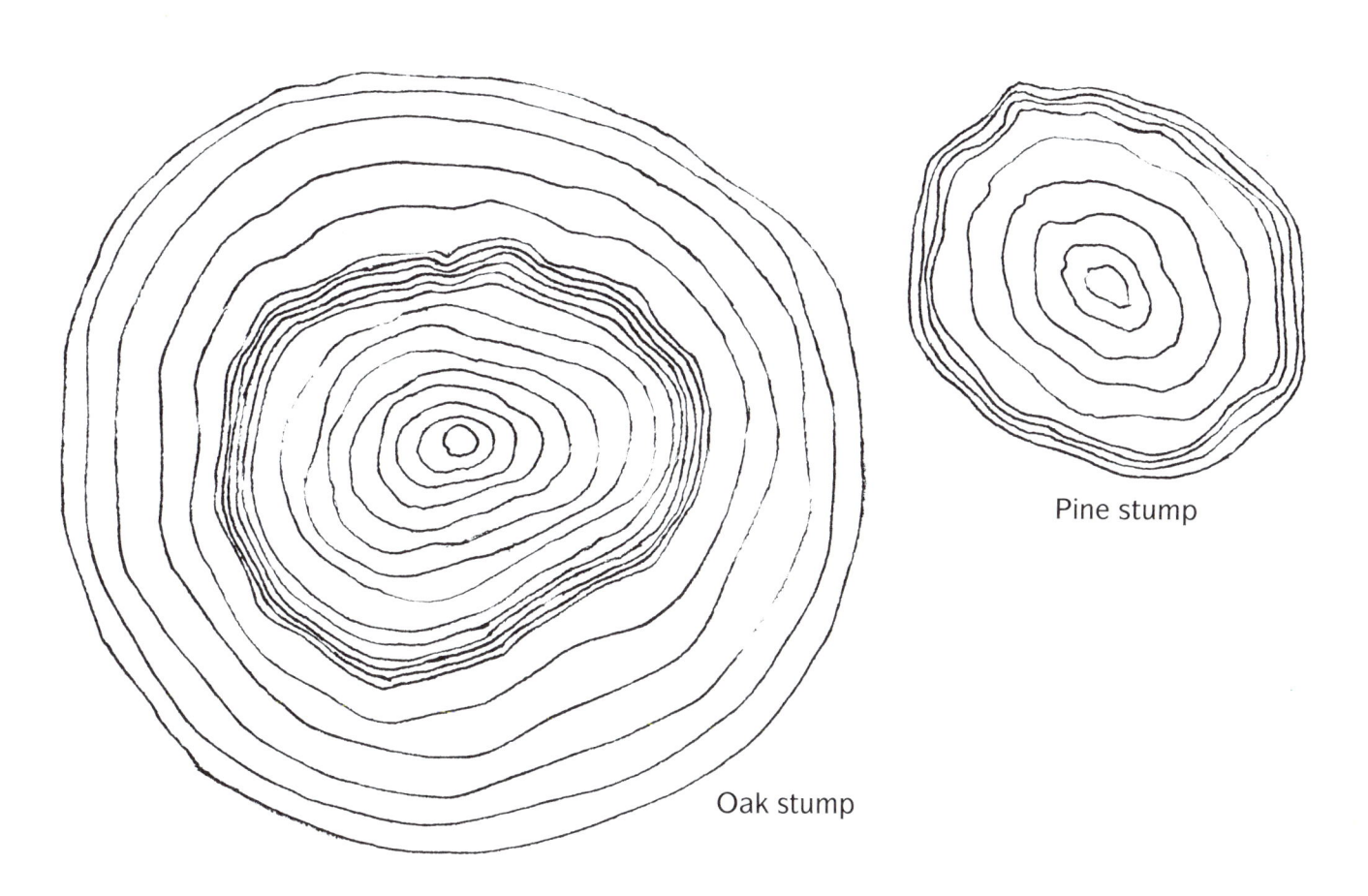

Pine stump

Oak stump

MAKE A BRANCH PUZZLE

In the spring you can usually find branches that have been broken off by winter storms. You can make a branch puzzle from a fallen branch. Try to find one about as thick as your wrist.

Ask an adult to help you use a carpenter or tree saw to cut the thicker end of the branch into seven or eight slices, each about an inch thick. Now mix up the pieces and see how quickly you can put them together in the right order.

Get a branch from another tree and make more slices. Mix together the slices from both branches. Can you still figure out how to put the two branches back together?

Challenge one of your friends to a branch puzzle contest. You put the pieces together first as quickly as you can. Then see if your friend can beat your time.

BARK RUBBINGS

The inside of a tree is protected by its bark. Unlike your skin, the bark on the outside is not living. But there is a thin layer of living inner bark underneath the dead bark.

Have you noticed differences in tree bark? Young trees have smooth bark, while older trees have rough bark. As a tree grows larger, the dead bark splits open to make more room.

Some people can tell a tree's name from its bark texture. Maple trees have smooth bark, and large white pines have crinkled bark. How would you describe the bark texture of trees near your house?

It is easy to make a picture of tree bark. You will need a dark crayon, some white paper, and someone to help you. Find a tree with interesting bark. Ask your helper to hold a sheet of paper on the bark while you rub the crayon briskly back and forth. Do not move the paper until the rubbing is done. Write the name of the tree on the paper if you know it. Make rubbings of several different kinds of tree bark.

BIG TREES

Have you ever seen a really big tree? Many of the largest trees in the world are in California. Some redwood trees are over 350 feet tall. Sequoia trees have the thickest trunks, sometimes over 60 feet around. It would take you more than 40 steps to walk around such a big tree.

Some states have big tree contests. They measure the trees' height, trunk thickness, and how far out the branches spread.

Is there a big tree in your neighborhood? Go on a big tree hunt. For measuring the trunk, take along a long piece of rope and a ruler.

Find a big tree. Lay the rope in a circle around the bottom of the trunk. Then pick up the rope until it is around the tree at your head height. Hold your fingers on the rope where one end meets the rest of the rope. Lay the rope on the ground and measure how much rope was needed to go around.

When you travel, look for other big trees. See if you can find one that measures more than 6 feet around.

ROCKS AND SOIL

SAND

Did you know that sand is made of little pieces of rock? There is lots of sand on ocean beaches, on lake shores, of and in deserts. You can find sand even if you do not live near an ocean or desert. There is always sand in the gutters along streets. This sand has fallen from trucks or has been washed in by rain water.

Ask an adult to help you gather a little sand from a road near your house. Carry the sand home in a small plastic bag.

Dump out the sand on a desk so you can study it. What different colors of sand grains can you see? Most white sand or yellowish sand is quartz. Silvery pieces of sand could be mica. Is there anything else in the sand that is not tiny rocks?

If you can get a magnifying glass, use it to look at your sand. Is most sand smooth or rough?

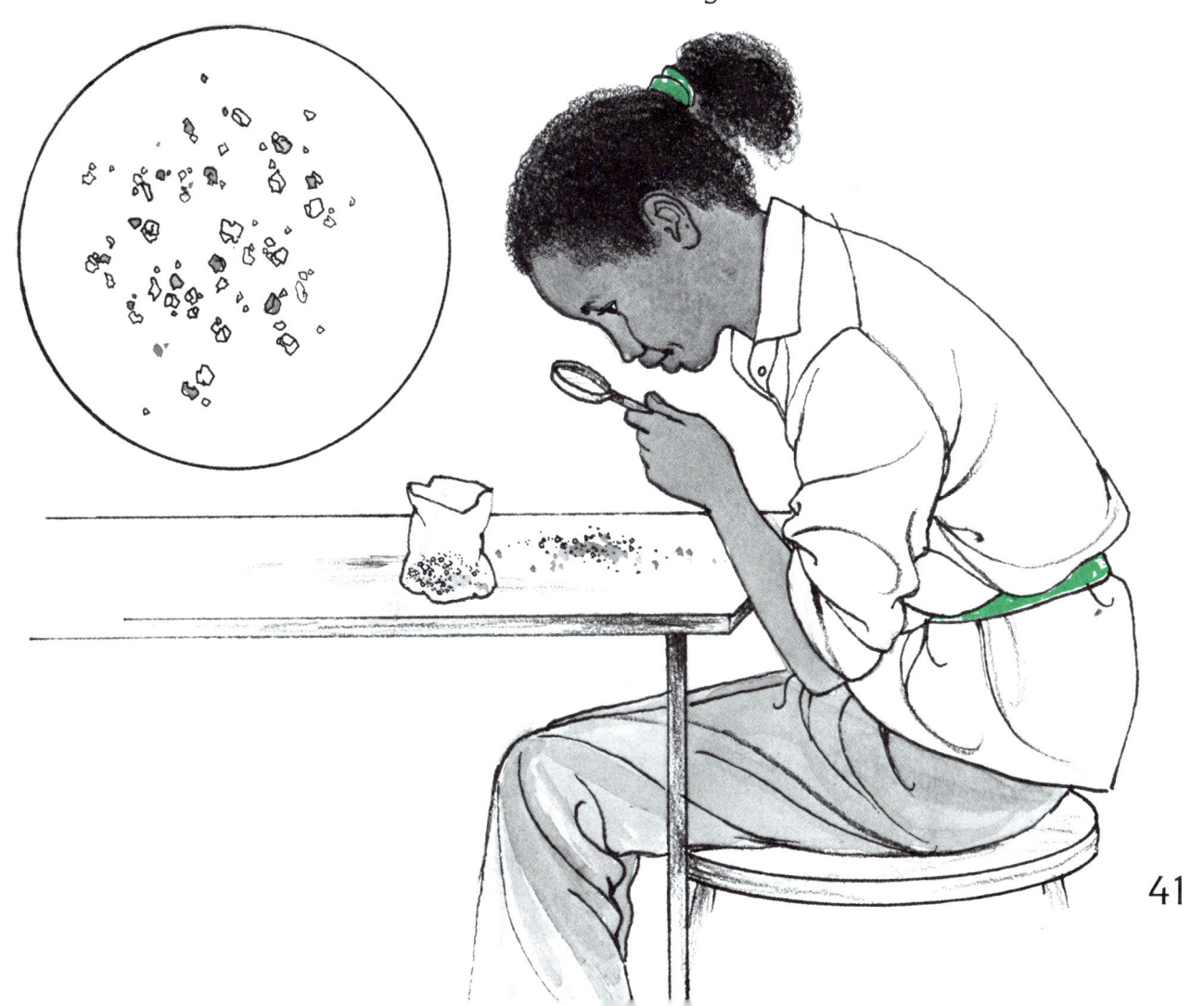

SOIL

Most people call it dirt, but *soil* is a better name. Soil forms when rocks are broken down into bits even smaller than sand.

Sometimes rocks are broken up by ocean waves or rushing rivers. In dry places, rocks are worn away by wind-blown sand. Even the sun and rain slowly make hard rocks crumble into soil.

You can make soil by rubbing together two rocks. Use rocks that are soft enough for you to scratch with your fingernail. You should be able to find a few soft rocks in the soil.

Hold the rocks over a piece of paper and rub them together. Push hard and grind off rock dust. Another way is to put one rock on the paper and hit it with the other rock.

Is it hard to make soil from rock? Think how long it took to make all the soil you see outside.

SOIL WATER

What else does soil contain besides crumbled rock? You probably know it has roots, worms, insects, rotting leaves, and pebbles. You may have forgotten that soil usually contains water.

Here is an experiment to find out how much water the soil can hold:

1. Get a large paper cup and fill it halfway with soil.

2. Spread out the soil on newspapers until it is dry. This probably will take several days.

3. Use a pencil point to punch ten small holes in the bottom of the cup.

4. Put the dried soil back into the cup.

5. Set the cup of soil in a bowl.

6. Fill a glass to the top with water, and use it to pour water slowly into the cup of soil. Stop adding water when it begins to run out the holes in the bottom of the cup.

7. Pour the water from the bowl back into the glass. The water that is missing has been absorbed by the soil. Is it more than you expected?

ROCK COLLECTION

There are rocks almost everywhere. You can make a nice collection with rocks you find outside.

One place to get rocks is from the soil. Search the bare soil along the sidewalk and under bushes. Most rocks are under the soil, so look for holes dug by people or bulldozers. Sometimes gravel driveways and walks have nice pebbles.

There are rocks along the edges of ponds and streams. Also, the department of public works (DPW) in your town probably has piles of crushed rock used for road building. Ask if you can take a few samples.

When you travel, pick up interesting rocks from places you visit. Watch for cliffs along a highway. Ask the driver to stop so you can gather a few fallen rocks. Remember, never go near a highway without an adult.

Keep rocks from different places in separate paper bags. Write on each bag the name of the place where you gathered the rocks.

Rock Data Chart			
Rock Number	Place Found	Properties	Name
1	Our garden	Soft gray	Shale ?
2	Our garden	Round Speckled	Granite
3	Gift shop	Purple crystals with points	Amethyst
4	Beach	White and Smooth	?
5	Beach	Smooth Speckled	?
6	School yard	Hard sharp edges	?
7			

When you sort out the rocks for your collection, give each one a number. The paper circles from a paper punch are the right size. Write small numbers on the circles and glue them to the rocks you want to keep.

How can you find out the names of your rocks? Your town or school library has rock guide books with pictures. Even with a book, however, it is often hard to identify many rocks. Maybe you can find an adult who knows enough about rocks to help you. If a rock is made of only one kind of chemical, it is known as a mineral.

Write information about your rocks and minerals on a chart. Include each rock's number, the place you found it, its description, and its name. Display your collection on a shelf or desk in your room so your friends can see it.

45

A NATURE MUSEUM

It is fun to visit a museum and see all the interesting displays. There are different kinds of museums for art, airplanes, antiques, science, dolls, and coins. You can have your own Nature Museum.

Here are some of the exhibits you can make when doing springtime science activities:

A collection of supermarket seeds;
A terrarium of little plants growing in a sealed jar;
A collection of bones found outside;
A collection of bones from your dinner table;
Plaster casts of animal tracks;
A tree branch puzzle;
Pictures of bark rubbings;
A rock collection;
Some weather instruments.

Arrange your exhibits neatly on a table or empty bookshelf. Write labels to tell a little about the displays. Then invite your friends to see your Nature Museum.

INDEX

Animals
    bone hunting and collecting, 22–23
    clues from eating habits, 26
    pond, 18, 19
    tracks, 24–25

Bigfoot, 14
Birds
    nest-making, 20–21
    seeds, 12
Bones, 22–23

Clouds, 32–34

Dandelions, 15

Flowers, tree, 35

Grass seed, 14

Nature museum, 46
Nests, bird, 20–21

Plants
    pond, 18
    seeds, 10–13
Pond life, 18–19

Rain gauge, 29
Rock collection, 44–45

Sand, 41

Seeds
    grass, 14
    sprouting, 12
    supermarket, 11
    transplanting, 13
    weed, 10
Snorkel viewer, 19
Soil, 42–43
Sponge, 14

Terrarium, 16
Thermometers, 28
Trees
    big, 40
    branch puzzle, 38
    flowers, 35
    rings, 36–37
    rubbings, 39

Water, 43
Weather
    clouds, 32–34
    rain gauge, 29
    station, 27
    thermometer, 28
    wind measurement, 30–31

Weeds
    dandelion, 15
    seeds, 10
Wind measurement, 30–31

ABOUT THE AUTHOR & ARTIST

David Webster teaches elementary science at two schools in Massachusetts. He was a staff member of the Elementary Science Study of the Education Development Center. Mr. Webster has written sixteen science books, including *Frog and Toad Watching* and *How to Do a Science Project*. The author lives in Lincoln, Massachusetts, and spends summers on Bailey Island in Maine.

Barbara Steadman studied at the Museum School of Art in Philadelphia and now lives in New York City. She illustrated the *Girl Scout Junior Handbook*.

LOCUST GROVE ELEM. LIBRARY

T 005434

DATE DUE

MAY 8					

HIGHSMITH 45-228